Made in the USA
Las Vegas, NV
27 July 2024

93029594R00085